Carillonneur

Also by Ágnes Lehóczky

ikszedik stáció (Budapest, Universitas, 2000)

Medalion (Budapest, Universitas, 2002)

Budapest to Babel (Egg Box Publishing, 2008)

Poetry, The Geometry of The Living Substance –

    Four Essays on Ágnes Nemes Nagy (Cambridge Scholars, 2011)

Rememberer (Egg Box Publishing, 2012)

Ágnes Lehóczky

Carillonneur

Shearsman Books

First published in the United Kingdom in 2014 by
Shearsman Books
50 Westons Hill Drive
Emersons Green
BRISTOL
BS16 7DF

Shearsman Books Ltd Registered Office
30–31 St. James Place, Mangotsfield, Bristol BS16 9JB
(this address not for correspondence)

www.shearsman.com

ISBN 978-1-84861-346-1

Set in Dante, with Fontin Sans titling,
and Myriad Pro prelims.

Contents

For our Sheffield times together....

Carillonneur

PART ONE

Parasite of Town

Greystones' Backyards

...through numerous lies this city unpeels its stratigraphy, by means of camouflage, by hiding, blending in long sequences of bus trips to and fro in late October rain between downtown and dark bricked alleyways. It's mostly iron rain, which streams down from the surrounding hills into the cracks of the concrete heart of this Northern settlement. When you do not know someone, like the way you don't know the intricacies of unfamiliar bodies, impenetrable ginnels, untouched geographies, you trust whatever they offer, allowing yourself to plunge into flooded impasses and cul-de-sacs, rivers of unknown neighbours' junk, cast-off children's toys, blown up rubber tyres, winter spades, ice axes thrown on the ground of hoarfrosty backyards' glossy ice rinks, wading through open doors of littered garages to lock your own bicycle in the shed. They offer you the post of the river diver to rummage through their junk. In this sense, there is no deception involved, since they too know riverbeds are thick, dense and grey. But sometimes they offer you more: liquefied maps with fuzzy street names to track down the old town which you can't quite touch yet with your mind. They often promise you a large number of rivers instead of the sea, hills instead of hazy dreams which they reckon are more tangible to climb. Or dive into. No gear needed to live here day by day apart from an oily anorak and a pair of old rubber thigh waders. But these rivers retreat into tiny arteries pulsing under the skin when you approach them. Then they offer you panorama. An afternoon through the kitchen window a solitary boy kicking a football within a square metre muddy grass knot or bizarre angles of tiny back gardens with the irregular visit of the odd guest who hangs their laundry out in the rain. So that you feel that you too should become a parasite on the carpet of this soggy cityscape. In the riverbed of this pale town. And accumulate clutter in your own cobbled courtyard. Two hours from London. Up towards the nucleus. Its whole life organised by its Northern aorta, the Pennines. According to the sign someone left in the underpass one day near Bramall Lane the sea must have been here a long time ago. And that's just possibly another lie too.

The Sheffield Mágus

Once when you visited this phantasmagoria land in the early days you highlighted its hideousness with no mercy in your manners, snapping pointedly at its malformed maps, the rough tarmac of heaving streets, solid houses with anaemic colours, the pre-cast and poured-in shapes of composites and wondered at the antonym of the word 'ostentatious'. We spent two days in the city sightseeing around trying to find the soft core of the spherical settlement, its delicate focal point, where, as you said, everything happens. Yet there is some raw untruth in every verdict. And sometimes it's the rawness that can pay some aphoristic tribute. These yellow, pink and lilac light effects at night enveloping the carcass of the city, erecting the outline of another ghost town, you established, are nothing but simulacrum. Silky legerdemain. Although under the multihued flesh of this city apparition a concrete caricature quietly clanks and clatters in the dark. In the daytime, from a bird's eye view if anything at all, the valley is industrious like an enormous workshop, a multitude of metal sawdust. But then it is the density of this iron debris, the valley filled with steel wool, copper wire, scrap aluminium items, which are magnetising. And we dived into comparisons with which we linked this geography to former and forgotten ones by mistake, from Bákó to Miskolc, Warsaw to Dunaújváros or Dresden... and then disappeared in the fluid afternoon through curvilinear glass pavilions of botanical gardens and fiery Guy Fawkes nights' crowded autumn fairgrounds, dizzying merry-go-rounds like the ones we'd seen at the edges of derelict seaside towns. Forgotten playgrounds which have crawled further inland to be closer to the core. The next morning you woke on the carpet, rolled up like a pupa on a pillow and a sleeping bag turned inside out to make the place habitable for me, you said. Yet you left in haste with the coach to London which was two hours away. The glossy window of the bus was black, like East Anglian flint or quartz reflecting nothing but the pallid complexion of the early morning station always already weary, with empty cafés, vacant corridors coated with white floor tiles still echoing from late night footsteps from the previous day. The day, you might say, has not started just yet and warned me to wait. I waited a few moments and dissolved into what you may call the wake of a city in a November morning or around that time.

Panorama from the Top of the Wicker Arches

Unable to find the delicate core, the focal point where everything happens, the streets led towards the margin of the city in that Saturday afternoon, sometimes between daytime and nighttime, not quite twilight yet, a few minutes past the difference between dusk and dawn, uncertain. Such day-fragments in January often blend into one smoky whirlwind of the hours sweeping tiny groups of women dressed in black, stacks of small and weightless twigs, towards home. Through littered roads wading in the debris of the day, they roll in air like ash or crows sweeping by metal shutters of shops semi-shut. An hour, in-between, when stallholders have nearly packed up all their goods, with only a few boxes of oranges, local eggs on sale still waiting to be sold. Then the fish smell. And the smell of disinfectants. The smell of small second-hand things. The tiny cafés with aluminium chairs piled up on the tables. We were standing here, I think, between a black bin and a yellow mop bucket, what I mean is between what actually happened and what could have happened to us in a half-existent here-and-now on the threshold of the urban market a few seconds before it was closed. That moment occurs when you arrive at an empty corner, not so much too late, but not quite right on time. The momentum of forcing an arrival on a space which is ready to depart, is what I mean by all this. And so we left with five small and ragged avocados, a cardboard egg box of six local eggs and one shiny Braeburn apple from some Yorkshire orchard. All at once blown out into the streets towards the district, where, you said, the Wicker began to stretch out into nowhere. To the edge of the heart. To the periphery where ghost kids kick phantom football and dark-clothed locals group at corners laconically nodding that they know how to inhabit this town without words. A spot which enables you to look at things from a distance but squinting from a distant enough distance sometimes allows you to fit every single miniature chip into a small but perfect pocket guide or map. And from the stone bridge over the watyr of Dune neghe the castell of Sheffeld we saw the angle of the city as if we had always been pilgriming in reverse, crawling backwards towards the core. We arrived in the empty streets in the end and stared into second-hand furniture shops and bric-à-brac boutiques with miscellaneous objects unreal and underpriced. Exhibits of a drooling vagabond in the window displayed between a metal kettle and a wooden nativity set with the thirteen characters still complete. Then following flocks of black skirts and scarves flapping in front of us in the wind we found the railway wall, the arch, the heraldic insignia carved out with a long peeled-off pride, a lion and a horse holding a shield *sola virtus invicta* but we thought this place was equally unconquerable and carried on walking wordlessly under the dysfunctional viaduct where, they said, in the odd hour one could spot blurred contours of cargo wagons of the Wicker crisscrossing the disused station and disappearing with the intermittent 'chuff' into the valley of no man's land. And then from the top of the forty-one invisible arches we saw the city from this twisted Eastern angle subdued under a weighty petrol-blue skyline, the city walls, the fire walls, the derelict factory surfaces, then the blind-glassed office walls, the enormous rounded gas tanks, unstrippable folios grown eclectically together, like fractured bones imperfectly healed, clumsily designed prosthetic limbs, mismatching mosaics of the afternoon hour in between, the pale palimpsest of now. We watched the tired posture of the landscape from this frame, paralysed in the hour where nothing really happens. And then we too got tired of staring at the littered streets, the deserted wide avenues dragging their way back to the plastered city hall wrapped in barbed wire (in its chronic battle with guano) and to the pinnacles of the two cathedrals each engaged in their own solipsistic monologue and decided not to return to the centre until we have exchanged words with those who, although so cunningly camouflaged, have colonized this peripheral segment of the world.

The Concrete Space: I in Heterotopia

[Leaving platform 5] en route to the South-West of the city where, I was told, everything happened, walking into twilight I got lost following the instructions of a cacophonous map, its clandestine directions written over one another. The horizon, I thought, is subterranean in this part of the world and likes to hide under layers of bitumen. Sky, which I last wandered under, was weightier than mud. This way it would be hard to find the way back to the dark bricked house, the corroded signboard 'Greystones Fish Bar' hanging on its firewall, to spot the Chinese man's old jovial face which for months now was a flag for some kind of homewards. His still expression under his white cap was like an accommodating anthropomorphic road sign semi-snowed up pointing toward the shaded, cluttered backyard sliced into two halves by the washing line cutting the tiny grassy patch into even tinier equal rectangular quotas the solitary phantom boy tended to plough through with his leather football each day after school ignoring any invisible border. But getting lost or drifting with the fluctuating crowd is much more artless than premeditated city meanderings. Allowing one to somersault impromptu into deep valleys and gutters, cracks of cobbled pavements tumbling down towards the bottom of a colossal gravel pit forgetting names of former cities for a while or letting their vacuums be flooded by the weiry Don. Absentmindedly consenting to early December to envelop them with thick snow. All tautologies attached to these discarded landscapes too become one thick layer of altocumulus mackerel sky, unpronounceable words I frequently mispronounced one day vanish in the winter whirlwinds of these driftings turning eventually into nothing but erased full stops. Geographically, so to say, missing the scheduled destinations and arriving at the unknown square I all at once rolled inside an enormous cementitious bowl like a kite pulled by a gravitational ghost semi-attached by the arm, magnetically drawn to the bottom of the basin rimmed with slopes unscalable, confined by seven chasms with never edge and crisscrossed by seven rivers undulating unnoticeably, like seven laundry ropes gone loose in the wind blending into a panorama always already fractured. I, in fact, felt as if she had found the soft focal point of the city, the square, like an asphalt lake shimmering in the middle of a concrete island, heaving in the late winter sunlight like a highway mirage, like a *délibáb*, felt suddenly familiar. Nither down, and they pointed at the open parade running backwards into the station after the first sudden afternoon snow fall, stretching between the invisible Porter Brook and the inaudible Sheaf, there once was a wasteland with a clandestine pathway hidden in the ground. What I saw now, they'd stroke the snowed-up horizon with a slow gesture of their palms, the wilderness bulldozed, the ghosts sunk deeper into the icy soil and a modern acropolis built on the top of the old tombland congesting any cracks and crevices through which I could have fled from this opaque land back to the country scaffolding vast skylines. And I noticed the slippery surface of the hillsides as if continuously rising higher like dough, the iced-up gloss of the concrete square which made it impossible to move fast on the pavement, the strips of frosty muck the locals dragged along on their boots in the strata of snow slowing them down as if they were astronauts walking on the Moon, or as if they were still connected with what was under snow, under sky, under earth via imaginary roots, their leather soles tunnelling phantom tunnels trudging everyday not so much on the tarmac of the streets but on some invisible borderline, thin *fata morgana*, or on some shaft of an old radio's signals, murmurs of an alternative map.

The Owls of Never Edge

And so to fabricate a city so unknown the telling lies continues. Never Edge is an undulating home of a street-lined deep valley without a rim. Beneath the earth's surface. It is because this valley must have been filled up by the North Sea a long time ago. According to the impromptu sign in the underpass near Bramall Lane. Despite the rumours of their mysterious disappearance from the landscape, two Tawny Owls live on the top of the foliage of the birches. You said they'd lived there for more than three hundred years. One day, a moment after nightfall they turned up out of nowhere, suspended on the starry skyline, wings so loudly flapping that they could have broken each other's frail feather bones. Both remiges and rectrices. It was impossible to tell whether it was a volatile act of lovemaking or a domestic tug of war or the intersection of the two but the two heavy bodies flew so intimately close to you, you said, that, entangled into one another, they shaped the grey face of the white-haired man who you were talking to at the sea one early summer evening. His stereoscopic eyes, where his eight wives, forty four children and a hundred and seven grandchildren dwelled, inspected you from an uneasy distance. His words, like the dozen of Honey Buzzards circulating around the church tower, flew out of his mouth high up in the air as far as the tiles on the roof twittering tales of the old graveyard over there, of the three thousand drowned sailors, the mad murderer and his two hundred Happisburgh virgins, all inhabiting the same cemetery. With a farsighted vision he carefully kept half an orange eye on the sky. But it is this forward facing piercing, this Northern light hunting which, you said, is a skill so useful to appropriate in order to find your way in a city so unknown. In the city of three-legged dogs. In order to have a vision which observes the planet with not eyeballs as such but with some kind of elongated tubes. To have disproportionately large eyes to decipher universes so disparate. And link them with half a blink. Or to separate overlapping earths. A large number of these solitary spectres seem to lurk in Ἀλβιών, bog men and bog women of the Isles, drifting from the North Pole to the South, from Aberdeen to Aberystwyth, from town to town, tavern to tavern humming or occasionally whistling the same song between dusk and dawn 'Tu-whit, Tu-who' to an anonymous *who*. You have heard this tune before, a long time ago, a mantra of an East Anglian ghost who stopped you in the Rose and asked about words. He asked how they sell. He was wearing a ten-gallon hat and smoked a cigar. Wingless. Or with very rudimentary wings. When you queried his knowledge he turned into a smallish urban fox. Small enough to puzzle everyone if there were a palpable threshold between prey and predator. A line to divide the scribe from the scribble. He then turned into an odd local who swore he had never said a word. He shut the pub door quietly after himself leaving only a tiny piece of fabric caught by the door. The corner of his coat. His unfinished and implausible tale. And remember the elderly actor with nicotine hued gaze, masked as the green man of the woods on one Midsummer Night who wanted to know about certain dates and places. He wanted to be your orbit. To make you converse. So that he could secretly erase the line between night and day. So that you would never go to sleep and too would become nocturnal. You seem to be bumping into these feathery phantoms, frail phoenixes of the past wherever you wander around this island. The veiled ghost of West Street, the Lindow Woman of this randomly designed map, was another one of them balancing on the metallic rails in the city centre late at night. Her eyes, two miniature lighthouses flickered from under her veil, two tiny table lamps blinking through net curtains. Yes, all these creatures must be anthropomorphologically related. The earth has only one topography at a time. It's one simultaneous pan-global event. Take the taxi driver, for another example, who winked back at you in the rear view mirror in Budapest and his anecdotes of the bank thieves who shot him in the abdomen nine times. He had nine lives like a cat, touch the sleeve of his winter heart. Not to mention the wordless drifter from Limerick, his dwelling place in the corner of the Bath Hotel permanent, in the city of three-legged dogs, unaccounted rivers, illusory owls. When the night turned to midnight he would nod a little and continue to scribble in his notebook without a sound... line after line, page after page, night after night, drink after drink, city after city, century after century, solar system after solar system... to whom... ho, ho, hoo-hoo-hoo-whoom...

Postcard from West Street

It's been many magnolia springs since the last time I lurked around that tree, so finely rooted in the middle of the lawn in the outskirts of Cambridge. You used to watch it from the window slowly changing its texture as years were unfolding casting shadows of the suburbs on your pale face smearing the colours of seasons on your skin... and although it's not May time yet when the magnolia tree blossoms puffy squabs which then fall by September on the ground like small bodies of dry moths, today's weather is already ahead of itself, winter here almost forgotten, a season *in advance*, just on the threshold of spring and I am up in the North far away from that spot under the wide open window where I used to stand between the tree and the white wall. Ordinarily, May arrives here more sleepily than in the horizontal Fens (you couldn't find two geographies more disparate), they warned me, we live higher in altitude and closer to the North Pole. And so within a hair's breadth of Aurora Borealis. The month next in line creeps in inch by inch, they told me, and so to learn to wear layers and not to forget to remember to change the clock tonight and urged me to start planning life according to the new time. I often hear of the most recent news in Ponds Forge which sits right next to Cobweb Bridge, on odd days nicknamed 'Flyover' dependent perhaps on the position of focal points, or the sun, the question of origin or the angle of squinting or spontaneity or collective seasonal mood disorder, I don't know. Resting with my elbows holding onto the tiled edge between two lengths from waist down dipped in the water with legs flapping like sea weed, half air and half water, sliced into two like a centaur, I looked at the perplexed hands of the giant central clock wondering who had untied the complicated network of an entire hour out of that late-winter Sunday evening, what mysterious air-breathing arthropod and I thought of the day shortened by three thousand and six hundred leap seconds and wondered if I had lost the edge of the season somewhere between the house in Crookes and the pool. And since swimming pools are the best places to unravel time or timelessness retracing the last zigzagging footsteps of winter I remembered the behemoth duvet cover I'd pulled on the hot radiator before I locked the door after myself then turned right at the corner of Netherfield Road somersaulting down seven chasms with never edge through Springvale to Taptonville Road via Winter Street straight into the spiralling Western Bank to find the heart of the city signposted by the colossal writing of the city's firewall drawing my memories fram somwher-elles to here arysyng fram shefeld cariage-place and shef-sqware to gon wandrynge abuten laberinthes of aere. I decided to learn this pictograph by heart reiterating every syllable until it made some sense, hieroglyphs which claim to have the magic power to decorate blank facades and inspire drunken teens in the middle of the night to slur each word and pondered hwat yf but I never thought surfaces can ever be blank. One needs to be a parasite gnawing through strata crawling with bright pupils under the skin of the many cities fossilised under plaster. To find the soft core, the delicate porous heart of the concrete. I pan over the erratic surface of maps every day to find the seven rivers entangling the city's heart like a wire greten and understonden hwat lyen abouten afore the cite wher dremen is re-paien the lives hwat lyen abouten as yit nat rede. But sooner or later unread lives and never written manuscripts, too, show through the topographic paper. That each map maker has their own vision of the absolute map. But there is a misplaced magnolia in every city, a lost bogeywoman lurking on every eclectic atlas and I thought of the lone soul I spotted the other night staggering on the tramlines shrouded in a long maroon veil. Her face cloaked with silk and secrecy, her two orange eyes gleaming in the dark. She'd be swept off to the side of the road each time a late night tram whooshed by throwing her right sleeve up in the air shedding random contents of her shopping on the rails. Then she'd thrust her body back onto the metallic lines like an amateur rope-dancer balancing with unfilled carrier bags in her hands. Meandering among honking cars her silhouette would again be blown back to the pavement by the next tram on its way to Hillsborough and so it'd go for about an hour, tautologically, with some obstinate but inexplicable intention, her shadow like an empty gown flying to and fro between the tram lines and the wall. Post scriptum. Tonight I thought I was by myself. I leaned my back against the house and stared into darkness, like a hooded courier with no news. (But they say these non-messages claim to have the power to predict the past.) I noticed a cat was staring me out in Crookes' dark backyard, curled up on the top of a brick like a perfect bean. The two eyes, light streetlamps, or miniature lighthouses, blind and blinding, watched my every step pottering around within the square mossy metre. It is a mild night. The sky is clear. Heavily starry. The hour is slowly turning to midnight. According to the new time.

PART TWO

Carillonneur

When Tremble and Tremor Turned up in Crookes

...everyone noticed how light the evenings became as the season turned, each time weighing less than a thousand grams. This meant that days were getting longer, filmier and time immaterial as if the town lived every hour next in line suspended inside an enormous, bronze palate over the grimace of Crookes' phantom hills. These circular days never reaching twilight gradually turned into cyclical sobbing, elastic equilibrium so the town could stay awake till total exhaustion or eternity. And although campanology of golden days still ruled, since all church bells had been long removed, town dwellers took on the task in turns. And the task was to impersonate time. And so they'd agreed on unconditional dictation: when a citizen's feet reached the ground, another was obliged to gesticulate, body vertical, upside down, mouth upwards. Clockwise. Anti-clockwise. Calling Tremble and Tremor, alternating lines. Basic vocal chords for enunciation without words. Exclusive guests from oval books, vocal encyclopaedias, unrecorded music sheets sat in the city's louvred windows. As if they were a goliath's miscellaneous souls. And the hosts of the town. Two Tawny Owls from Nether Edge and two Papillons. Then two sobbing toddlers in pushchairs, a nurse, and her postman husband, too. These first summer evenings in the city refused to darken, the sun to lower any further. An illuminated era of never-ending balls and banquets multiplied into countless festive courses, leaving light bulbs flickering all night long, bazaars and antique shops open, merry-go-rounds going round and round, taps dripping, bell clappers swinging and the season rising between dusk and dawn so the neighbours could get no sleep. An extravaganza for the globe's most elegiac, bell-free settlement. A real carnival, a gala of gargles and gurgles, the festival of the human tongue. And there were other rules too which forbade participants to copy, plagiarise or to repeat combinations already performed, in any shape or form. And the goal was a bona fide exchange of thoughts about the correct hour. By visuals, signals, gestures, writing, by any decadent behaviour except by speech. Which meant one had to improvise a new story about the eternal city (built on seven muddy hills) each time it was one's turn. The nights were so bright you also had to close the shutters. It was meant to be the longest day; as long as it would last. Twenty-four white hours spent in Tawny Owls' large, byzantine presence. With wine and Scottish salmon upper- and underground. And a damp yard where those uninterested in the games could have a puff. (This wet landscape happened here a lot, those low skies' aluminium taps often flooding flora and fauna, saturating cobbled backyards. O the soaked patios. Small, miscellaneous districts of the word atlas. The absolute wetmap marked with no margins.) But the premeditated civic discourse turned out to be a paradox. A failure, almost fatal. The conversations. Clockwise. Anti-clockwise. The acrobatic attempts to kill or measure time. It was impossible to be a courier tugging on real news. As if tugging on plugholes of unpluggable seas. Being pulled and dragged out tongueless from this bric-à-brac land. Which meant it was ill-advised to synchronise, too. This meant you had to be *you*. So it soon turned into a *solo*-symphony contest in the end. And each performance had its own eclectic but idiosyncratic design. Tremble needed to negate Tremor's mind, though both at the same time wondering why all metal resonators had fallen silent in the region. And replacing the accuracy of golden town clocks, at what price could Tawny Owls make time move forward on the shimmering horizon. Heads twitching, beaks screeching (or hooting). Calling up, then calling down. Three to treble. Five to two tenor. Three to lead. The necessity of separating *who*'s voice from the crowd. To study anatomy: of the lips, the teeth, the tongue and the hard palate. The architecture of the mouth. And since harmony was not one's goal, it soon turned into a fierce cacophony, a competition of the throats. Then the confusion as to whose turn it was to say the farewell first. But campanology's old rules ruled once more. And since palates could memorize musical patterns, even the acoustics of the unpronounceable, what was said was said many times so it was impossible to tell whose the original line was. And the guests preferred hearing them only once. You were not meant to articulate the same constellation twice. The two Papillons and the toddlers in the pushchairs were already gone. When Tremble and Tremor ran out of words to gesticulate they poured themselves another see-through Pinot Noir. In order to forget fear. It was called lexophobia. So they cleared their clogged-up throats and picked a tightly clustered dark purple pine cone bunch of grapes for the next journey. They held it under their tongues. For the taxi ride in the middle of the brightest midnight. Those glasses they drank from were tarred with lees, they motioned in the end ready to leave the city's phantom street where black cabs never stopped. Searching for the secret ginnel down to the Southern hemisphere. The clandestine path back to the earth's focal point. Time to ship their red suitcases across the ocean to unknown peninsulas. When you go, the disillusioned neighbourhood snapped, make sure you don't leave that giant metal body in the middle of the city. Smuggle the hundred tons of nuisance across to an alternative home. Take your acrobatic attractions away on your back, how else? But it was believed that the earth was shrinking nonetheless and one day in the end all distinct silhouettes, outlines of hieroglyphs, days, seasons, topographies, shadows, contours of iron bells, chords, colourations and continents, in fact all cacophonies would merge into one boundless sound. And they looked in the bottom of the bottle, up in the circular ceiling, and saw what one had owned became very blurred. And that blurred was beautiful. Denizens freq-uently confused the typography of those two verbs and ended up being lost or in debt. Tremble and Tremor were meant to stay and write an alternative composition, the crowd would try to reason, of a city where there are no clock towers to count the hour. Planets don't overlap. Bodies are heavy and immobile. They weigh more than a ton. That's more than twenty hundred-weight when you are falling downwards in the room from tops of tall towers and campaniles. It was always meant to be an impromptu opus. The structure, the logic, the constancy. The query of the *who* whom you had been talking to all this time. There is one last thing to do, the failed orchestrators mumbled, so the city should try a new method; some serious, scientific tuning. An alternative acoustic exercise. It requires focus, fidelity and fearlessness, they added. The task is to free souls of long-forgotten zoos out of your throats. Imagine, Tremble and Tremor gestured, the absolute harmony when you force the locked open. All the miscellaneous melodies of the planet never played before. Bizarre creatures from the shelter, ones with three or four legs, or ones which stretch the fourth one backwards to look like a tail, ones which could sing and guard your thresholds. Ones as large as wolves or lycanthropes, with both eyebrows meeting at the bridge of their noses, curved fingernails, low ears and swinging stride, ones which could strip off their old skin when the winter comes and hanging it on old trees disappear when your fears flame up like a torch. But there is no threshold in this city between the thought and the said, only invisible rivers. And there is a difference between howling and music. Music is what makes one sob. Howling is just annoying. They could howl at the full Moon or the Midsummer Sun as a response to late night sirens. Another house was on fire that night. One must dine quickly and quietly and then order a cab, they nodded and stood upright. A black car, which at cataclysmic times like this, turns up without a siren and drives wordlessly like a ghost from the middle of the thousand and one white nights to the starry nowhere. A cab without making any irritating noise. One must call for a vacuum of absolute silence just after past midnight with a driver whose lips are sewn together so he cannot say a word. To leave the table with the vocabulary of nothing in the mind.

Walkley's Viola

At noon, in the beginning of October, my late autumn guest, the drifting carillonneur with a name unpronounceable, who moved from one cobbled corner of the city to the other every time the season turned, looked out of the louvred window and stated that no-one rings church bells to signify the hour in Walkley anymore. In fact, she added, if this grey cloud had set in 'now', it would stay above the city, and what's more, it would dwell in the chasm of the valley perhaps, for an unpredictably long time, for eternity. Look at that gigantic arc of humidity stretching between Walkley and Hillsborough, a perfect and multicoloured crescent above the city, above the earth. But just before one's mouth could shape a frail 'oh', the vision vanished, and one wondered if all that had just happened was in fact at all true, if the bands one thought one saw were merely artefacts of the photopigments in the eyes. But there is truth in evaporating contours of bridges, she said, there is truth in the vacant, the hollow, just dare stare into the midst of the fog. It is the borders of such densities couriers are to cross, the day's outlines after the rain, the hazy contours of the Hillsborough hills. It's such a day which ends abruptly and you too fall into an inexplicably opaque mood forgetting what then you called 'magic', the perfect portico made of air and basic colours. Look, she said, it's that kind of unexpected 2 a.m. which shakes and then wakes you; when your face looks pale and puffy like small planets, have you, she shook me, have you been shaken like this before? In a room that's dark and empty and no-one else is around. Except on the semi-lit pallid wall, there's always a shadow swinging, limbs and empty sleeves, a silenced body of a bell. The body: an anonym messenger, the corpse of a postman, the remains of a fallen archangel. And my guest, like a tongueless psychopomp speaking several inaudible tongues, continued quietly. If the city's focal point vanished in fog, she said, and there are no contours left to cross, you could always throw a stone at a hooded crow (straight from Eurasia) to see—if the stone, or pebble flew over the sea you would become a vagabond forever; if it landed on a building, she said, they said you could put your anchors down. Buildings gaining and losing significance as seasons change are so much like the word *you*. And all *yous* are like defunct trams that used to run on schedule from here to town and back. But then ghost trams are very much like mute bells, from the convex eventually morphing into the concave, or from the hollow to the convex, my nameless guest added, and wondered when this eternal curse on carillons would be revoked. For without them cities forget how to count time. Let's walk in and out of Walcas Leah this mid-October Sunday, she said. At noon. Walkley is renowned for celebrating Sundays without a sound, in fact each Monday, and what's more, each day carved out of the calendar seems to turn into an eternal silent Sunday in this part of the planet. But it seems no colour can stay the same for longer than a split second. These autumnal shades resemble contours of unexpected guests who leave the dinner table in between two courses and with an intermittent 'chuff' disappear into the valley of no man's land. One day you'll need to find those iridescent tracks to be able to find your way backwards in the season, she warned. The more erratic the route, the closer you are to *you*. You could choose, for instance, the closet path by the boarded up Netto which sits anonymously on South Road like a dysfunctional gesture, a building ready for dark November weekdays. That is Sundays, in Walkley. People should ring knells, she said solemnly, for departing buildings like that. Eventually they will always open their shutters. The other evening, she nodded, she saw a thin shaft of light squeezing through the metal blinds when a quiet workman stepped outside to light a cigarette in the rain. These unnoticeable crevices. The small and absent spaces between the bric-à-brac. Your name isn't Echolalia, she insisted. You are not the bog woman of the margin. One needs to travel relatively far in order to be remembered all at once at an impromptu corner of a familiar street; one needs to be loyal to tap random shoulders gently and be just generally merry about meeting *you* again. But you don't meet anyone in Walkley. South Road is quiet with few, empty shops. Their shelves haven't much to offer other than packages of rice and a few odd home grown courgettes. There is a butcher. And a charity shop no-one dares to enter. If I knew your address, she leant closer, I would write down a list of second-hand items on a postcard and post this postcard on a Sunday. The catalogue of objects which smell like second hand things. A Hitchcock DVD and a porcelain tea set. A pair of worn shoes. An old viola. But there isn't a post office in Walkley. One easily becomes absorbed by these faithful compasses, redundant references when staring them out through the steamed up window on Sundays, when no-one is there to watch. We must go back and remember an extra second hand item and scribble the name down on the list. Today the new item is the skin-coloured viola. With no price tag. Priceless, I mean. People don't buy presents from these shops anymore. It's because they smell of old people's wardrobes. I would buy you the viola, if you were closer. Walkley is within vicinity. Let's crawl an inch closer to the charity shop window and see if someone left an old pendulum in one of the dark corners. And stare into chipped flakes of unframed mirrors. Did you know that hooded crows are the only birds who can recognise their own reflections? A pair of binoculars leaning by the porcelain tea set; glasses clouded with past Sundays' fog. This vicinity is what one's always intrigued about. I don't know Walkley, but I do know you, she said, and looked into the binoculars, pointing the two barrels at my face. I could pretend Walkley is *you*. I have glued a guardian angel to every wall of every single chamber within the vicinity of Walkley. Within these Victorian walls. Someone said there is not one straight line in these buildings. If you were to place a marble on the floor it would scroll down in one direction and end up in the opposite corner, like one's random thoughts. One's unsaid longings to hear *you* again. To follow the ball's route into unknown corners where spiders dwell. And finally decide whether to allow these air-breathing arthropods to dwell near *you* or to hoover them up into a tongueless vacuum. And send them off to the realm of Echolalia. Walkley is a place of no importance although it does have a name. One shouldn't be jealous of things which echo a name. Name is vicinity, she said, and boredom. Which makes you wonder who it is who matters. The personal paradigms, the private patterns of one's auto-geographical charts. I have not designed this topography yet, and she threw a blind map on the kitchen floor, a white sheet, with the absence of cul-de-sacs and unnamed guests who come and dine and leave just about midnight without a word. She said she was told Walkley is a large garden made up of many mazy gardens. That there are sixteen minutes between Walkley and the hills, uphill. 'Sixteen eternal minutes', between now and then, between the thought and the said, they would always add. You could try throwing bones instead of stones into the vacuum of the valley. Imagine what these alternative citybooks would be about, mapped by a hooded botanist of pavements: about secret detours of the wolves of Walkley, patterns of the rain of Walkley filtering through old calcium of bones, peripatetic wonders of midnight Walkley, nocturnal tunnels of the wind of Walkley. I think this is what they would write. It's Sunday eve and the route from here to *you* is risk; a blindfold journey between two random thoughts. Between the body and the ink. They would write it here. Let's pop down the street to look again at the charity shop items. One day those items will be priceless and no-one will want to stay at home. Let's see what those second-hand things look like in the dark. Through the dusty glass. When no-one is around. That night I took the shadows of the hanging laundry off the wall. The hangman wearing a white terrycloth gown was gone from the room. On odd days I wonder if I had taken it to the charity shop. My guest, whose name was unpronounceable, vanished too with the howling of bewildered bells. The following night only tiny dark leaves flickered on the white. I spotted the viola leaning next to the Hitchcock DVD. The street was wet after a brief October Sunday shower beating against the window for about half an hour. Soaked panorama of soft hills. You could watch it for hours and simply just say and remember nothing the next day. And think of other places you could fluently write about. This, a ghostscape of the mind. The Indian shopkeeper told me the other day. They buried Walkley under tarmac. Tonight Walkley is cut into two halves by the Moon. You could maybe write about another Walkley. The alternative yous of Walkley. Other hours of Walkley. Let's meet on the corner Walkley. And say this is where we met. Exactly at noon. Tapping shoulders. You must've heard of Rivelin before. The rainbow arching above houses across the valley holding Walkley and Hillsborough tight up in air, holding together the two poles of the earth under one name. Under one enormous silenced sound. Late October wind of Walkley. Secret detours of the wolves of Walkley. Wet weather of Walkley. Sobbing Sundays Walkley. Fearful secrets of charity shop Walkley. Quiet butchers of Walkley. Spotted dogs tied to lamp posts in front of greengrocers Walkley. If Walkley were *you*, I could make more sense. Let's look into the bottom of the sink; if you look close enough, there is a small insect staring back at you with telescopic bright eyes, rudimentary wings soaked in soap. Where have we left this conversation. In air. I have lived here all my life, someone said at the bus stop the other day. Wait, then. The catalogue of second-hand items. The deep voiced viola. The stone, staying up in the air stuck above the fogged valley like an iron bell clapper muted, frozen in the middle of swaying.

The Carillonneur's Song

Ye bells of forgotten belfries, damp Hillsborough bedsits. There is no word out of this labyrinth. Small spiralling spaces of forgotten foundries, mouldy firewalls drowned in thick January fog. A hazy afternoon when I took that sleety route towards Wereldesend. The border between Neepsend and Owlerton, and rolled down the bottom of Herries Road to Wordsend. The day hid under the shadow of icy Shirecliffe. A so-called Tuesday, a no-name picked from an antiquarian's old *A to Z*. At an irrelevant address in a random cobbled street no-one ever turns into (so many of them in this part of the world). An unremembered circuit of a day-trip stretching between two poles of a breath. One which one must intimately utter to fill in the void in memory one day when one sits down to learn these random routes by heart. Trudging through an unmemorable map. By a colossal hollow furnace. A defunct railway which ceased to run in the midst of journeying across this January landscape. Under a grey rainbow of twenty-four hours pending above the earth. A single day patroned by St Zero. St Nil. A stalactite suspended in the frozen mid-air in the middle of drooling from my mouth. They say that the first who was buried in this land was to be the sentinel. The spectre. Destined to guard this silent settlement for ever. With some inexplicable sentiment. The fifteen-year-old blonde boy, I wondered. The adolescent Ann Fish. The keeper of lost and forgotten items, litter of urban caves, heaps of rubber tyres dumped in the small vacuums of valleys. The guardian of bobbly sofas of the planet stuck in the mud every hundred yards all along the river. Looking after nooks and crevices, heaps of light bones. Of the small and fictitious creatures of the woods. Minnie Clarke's remains, Ada Meeson's limbs. The drowned Ernest Gibson's. The tiny bones of the twenty-four letters of the charity shop. Ye bells of forgotten belfries, there is no day out of this calendarium. Sooner or later, pigeons will occupy outer space. They'll perch inside invisible nooks of bells, watch towers, clogged-up cul-de-sacs; coarse throats of dovecots, cooing with no consequence. (That night a horde of wild boar passed by dark firewalls quietly, in a line, slow caravan of dark bodies stalking under the Moon. There were seven of them. On the periphery of the city, at the edge of the urban night they vanished, right into the middle of the black woods of the Buda Hills. Then. But not now.) The goal was to find the definition for another unknown day. A long time ago I knew someone in this city who lived with a bronze bell in the garret, the size of a carillon, silent, soundless, with a withheld resonance of a brief metallic breath, like the numb tongue of a tiny old woman who has no strength left to sigh a single sound except a name, which weighs less than a thousand grams. A street name from an old *A to Z* scribbled on a tag. Olivia. Ann Fish. Antoine. Elisabeths from dusty antiquarians. A day with no marks by anonymous scribes in the January calendar, the pigeon feeder hummed into my ears. Ye bells of filthy columbariums. Bells of belfries. No architecture can escape pigeon shit. The foul, unfinished pages. Graffitied Hillsborough ginnels. The guano globe. But the question, he urged me, is whether you had the courage to take a seat in the bobbly armchair stuck in the muddy landscape waiting till dawn for the river to flood, for the body to float, for all the rubber tyres to swim up to the surface. (Not that they were not visible before.) The Danube, it was. The river Don. The litter. The letter. There is no separation between words in the end. They weigh the same weight. The fossil. The father. The soul and the soil. I should make my mind up. Whether what I saw was a valley or a void filled up with inner or outer space. And the day, like a tiny rectangular canvas on strings, slowly took to the air. I was holding onto the frozen arc of the twenty-four hours, the twenty-four letters of the charity shop, the tiny bones of the twenty-four talismans of friendship in my pocket, pulling the strings back with my own calcium skeleton, hideous puppets macabre. Ye bells of forgotten belfries, there is no compass out of this catalogue. If you leant close enough, the garreteer said with a creased soul, pressing his ear against the bronze chest, you could hear it was out of breath. More precisely, as if it were breathing spherically. Inward: a circular ride on the giant wheel held high in the frozen air like an unknown name from the world atlas of a deceased world, rotating as if it were a small facsimile earth around the Earth. You the sentinel. The first one to be buried in this settlement destined to love this mudscape for ever. St Nil. Poor Mary Ann Fish. People become wordless when they are most eager to speak, the bell bearer said. The word, the rememberer. And all that matters is the victory of one's weight, of the height, of the whole body's resistance. O vertigo. O the neglected anniversaries of all lost items in the world, of all litter of urban caves, of every single letter in the alphabet. Of all still-born sounds. One day they'll regain their old shape in the January fog. Ye bells of forgotten belfries, damp Hillsborough bedsits. Broken drain pipes; mouldy January dawns trapped in hollow foundries. I took a seat on the bobbly sofa stuck in the middle of the mud and turned my head towards Wereldesend like a Hooded Crow, the one who flies into this country all the way from Eurasia. And when you were gone I counted quietly: the fifty horses, the thirty-eight cows, the eight donkeys, the two hundred pigs and fowls and the seventy-two tame rabbits. The thousands of scratch marks on the inside. The twenty-four small skeletons of friendships. All the telegrams of the Earth sent out underground while we were alive. All the lost and preserved manuscripts. But this happened a long time ago. Whoever drifted this way had to become the sentinel of the settlement for ever. Someone who actually picks up the phone. St Zero. The sexton. St Nil from the old *A to Z*. From the catalogue of the uncountable. The guardian of all unaccounted items of the earth. And I took a mouthful of air from the circular landscape and held it for a long minute as if one could have colonized it for a split second with one breath.

And true. The hillside was already a rabbit warren. I ran off into the woods behind the Hillsborough Barracks into the Buda Hills. I balanced on the derelict rail line between Manchester and Budapest. Between the Danu and the Duna (the most polluted river of this island), between two real obelisk ghosts. What makes this void walkable in the end is the stubborn overgrowth of Japanese knotweed. The only way out of the bogland, the dead ringer shrugged his shoulders, might be to think of something of the unconditional. Something of the boundless, the absolute. And a moment later he was gone. Then I took a sharp change in altitude, and passing by the giant telegraph pole I ran across the bridge to find the exit. The entrance. The definition for an unknown word. I tapped a stranger on the shoulder on my way out to see if she remembered the day when we had met. What will be written on your epitaph, she asked and pointed at the ragged sofa floating on the Don. Which was not the Danube, she was certain. This river is in Werledsende. The worn out mattress on her futon, she argued, already felt like a grave. And George, the stranger's old collie turned up suddenly, too, with a pelvic bone in his jaws from behind the wobbly tombland. An old Roman helmet. The skull of tiny Ann Fish. And we looked around the land. Tautologies of the planet's discarded blackened condoms along the path were meandering towards the heart of the city. The rows of shanty towns on tops of nameless hills. Lost in the lack of fauna and flora along the barbed wire fences. The vegetation of nothing. The reiteration of early morning dog-barks. The number of dusty lycanthropes howling through those barbed wire fences into the world. We came here to find an architectural ghost. To track down some unknown family tree; bare and Beckettian with black wet boughs. This cemetery didn't survive on the map. And yet stretching miles out towards the West. Yes those tombs always looked quite ready to get up and go. It is the angle they lean in at. And the moving earth underneath. It's the obsession with the bleak, the new sublime. What's fog in your mother tongue, my new companion finally wondered at the end of the January drift. That stuff that chokes the objects, that creamy substance which envelops one's face with nothing. That drains the voice. It's just an ad hoc item from the catalogue of unplanned cosmic events, I thought. A *chance* word, a transparent name filled with infinite space I wanted to shout into from the top of the Hillsborough hills.

PART THREE

Phantom Poems

The Chronicle of a Leap Day

Don't be anxious. Read time from the phantom calendar. Account for fugitive hours. A parabola drawn between that which might be and that which could have become. Understand the ellipsis between equinoxes, cities, alternate breaths which know nothing about each other. The history of air inhaled unmatches the oxygen ejected. And we all know that. It's impossible to superimpose the two. They say those who live by itinerant dates can't inhabit a square millimetre in either a necropolis or an acropolis (oh you leapling...). The mind of an hourglass thinks supplement moments so that the cycle works, the solar system functions. Astronomical events seldom repeat themselves. Stillness is drifting. Cities crawl out onto memoirs' margins. Trespass their own limitations to be *somewhere else.* There is static in the riding of a magic carpet. Holding onto the mane of a word. A name, the arc, which holds the hemisphere together. One's life balances on the absolute map, once you thought. A long time ago. But the lifetime of the word also depends on air between unsynchronized, lunisolar heart-beats, or a tiny whirlwind of geomagnetic draught caused by a turning page. Something quick, comma-sized, occurs along the diameter of a frog's goliath leap. Look. There is nothing else to do. There is some good in blinking into the last rays of winter sun. You might go so far as to call it love.

Post Scriptum

This summer, the bill-clattering white storks (birds of the year), the news said, are preparing to migrate ahead of time. It's hard to get unaccustomed to such advances. Study the stars, you reiterate every summer. Gravitate more towards another earth. Decipher the chronicles of the microcosmos. You could always move your arm and neck in a way that pokes upwards into Andromeda fog. Dark matter. Keyhole in the universe to peep in on others.

The Ornithologist

Remember a woman who   one winter night remem-
bered a woman whom she didn't know   who remembered
a woman she didn't know   who remembered   a woman
who remembers memoirs of a woman she knows nothing of.
She opens a white camper van   and enters   the nest   of
another dark   soft knowledge   woven from distant
woods.   She feeds the coal burner with coal and climbs into a
goliath's head and all night pecks at tapestries   remembering
a woman she didn't know   who remembers a woman   whom
she knew nothing of.   This nothing was a tiny green – or
blue –   canal boat moored on a phantom map.   The
carpet. Her thick black hair.   The mane of a nomadic name.
Untameable.   In the morning it was just everywhere.   And
then the twist and turn till dawn next to her. In such a way
that by the time she woke   she'd forgotten unremembering.

Post Scriptum on Superimposition

Hold onto the old binoculars. Only one telescope works. You could always point towards the blue Moon. Learn to adjust. Collimate hazy horizons. Align atlases of the self.

November Short-Cut

meet you in the Stag tonight the anonymous text read a short-cut through winter via Frog Lane an alley that exists on the map only if you dare doubt it if you venture into that province render yourself invisible so that you stand out in other words a poor aporia unremember the mausoleums of Sharrow and the mouldy micro-climate of their rooms corners congested with hooded muggers concealed rivers dirty vans parked in the same spot forever because they say that something quick a rushed tête-à-tête an agile clause an ad hoc desire to converse failed and stuck in air repeats itself in the pattern of graffitied streets chequered rooftops soot-skinned firewalls drifting from catacomb to catacomb torso to torso skin to skin erasing past arrangements made on pocket maps the nighttime dérive of a collector of street names the tomb raider of nomadic leavings or longings who frees you from familiar addresses safely stamped on the atlas of your mind the second-hand items no-one's ever owned it's not who runs or who desires snow slows you down the event is in the things escaping objects oscillating the contours of an unfound name and look the world blurs into dusk and the absent stand out like language suddenly palpable and snow just everywhere all elements carry the same heavy fog weight tons of smoke or ash say you could think with the mind of an hourglass the convex and concave forms of breathing you might go so far as to call it killing time

Post Scriptum on the Speed of Forgetting

Try to think of something conclusive, she urges. The swift detour people take, or the speed of their streamlined thoughts of departures. Of back doors which suddenly swing open, the fearful speed with which an urban falcon twitches her head, the acceleration of summer, as it exits and leaves us with the terracotta floor of a dried up lake. Dead ducks in small heaps, cast-off clothing, a telegrammic beer bottle; the only convex items on the flat horizon after such a topographic stun. (Or the other way round. Think of the subliminal. The cowering dry grass knots, once overflowing litter bins shrinking, the decline of dehydrated willows, the concave, indifferent about duration; and below, the slow time of the sandclock's bulb.) And the timeless in between; the migrating swallows which after a long hour of silent gathering on electric wires cutting the continent in two exit history early morning without a hint or the smallest sound of the flap of a wing. And it is not a threat. The concave's bound to become convex. But if only you could think of a word with the race of light to forget the metropolis fast which, year after year, metamorphoses without you.

The Ecology of Air Corridors

You always measure yourself in relation to the cosmos, the armchair astronomer said. Down there, she pointed with her index finger on the map on her lap, *terra firma*, space's largest necropolis. The orb: an urn of calcium. A terracotta pot of palimpsest of imploded mindscapes. Stare out of your citadel and squint at the oval Moon. Then down there, at the miasmic Earth. Adjust. Collimate drifting atlases of thoughts which know nothing about thinking. We were flying above the city encircled in fog evading other planes and planets suspended in the Northern hemisphere unable to land due to severe weather conditions in Budapest. Anticipate cataclysm, the paper says, she warned. Think of the falcon family perched on the top of St George's relentlessly pecking at the map of their nest. The totalising eyes, the lack of knowledge. The non-response to passing apocalypses. And imagine you are safe. A thought throbbing on satellite. Study the philosophy of fog. The halo where bodies end and others begin. The intimacy of borders. The vocabulary of the edge. The marginalia of air corridors which make no sense on earth or in the air. Find an illuminated name for an unnameable airport and allow this name to land on its own hoarfrosty tarmac.

Post Scriptum on Mud

And the condition of happiness is in the correlative. I mean in the relation of lack. Pick the two most random from the round mass of objects which know nothing about the nature of mirrors. No such things as parallels. Only one giant spidersilk canopy. Rounded in unutterance. Study the physiology of frogs, the life lived in a toxic environment, the capacity to leap away (from clattering red beaks, the beaks of the year), the distant vision, the state of torpor, the centaur mindscape, half clay, half fluid, and then the swift hesitation whether to belong to earth or liquid or in-between.

On the Cadence of Forgetting

'The only time I visited the city, many years ago, I was stuck in a hotel room in winter, sick and delirious, overlooking the Danube with vast blocks of ice floating down the river while Laura went out to try to find some pot noodles or dried soups from some garage still open. And so, having nothing else to do', she writes, 'I read'. The folio of fog. The final hours of the last day were oppressed by low-lying clouds in Franzstadt. The grey mist rose from the riverbed crawling above fin-de-siècle courtyards, via lichtofs to the tops of giant furnaces stripping the Market Hall of its coloured tiling, the firewalls of the Mills of their soft sepia. It haloed the silent Slaughterhouse, erasing the pigmentation of the Habsburg iron bridge (with its bronzed falcon long flown off). The trams, scanned, oxidised, exited time. The riverbank disappeared from the map trafficking every little black dog from along the public paths all the way to *no*where. The sun right above the bridge died out like a gas ring, the way the contours of those pale inhabitants, unnotified *flâneurs* also slowly bled away in a phantom Europe. The old year's unpublished account of what might have occurred in the here-and-now before. This, you could call, a new year's resolution.

Post Scriptum on Symbols

Postmodern men and women, the scholar says in between two courses (between the fish soup and the stuffed cabbage), burn much longer these days in crematoria, from the quantity of E numbers they stuff down their throats. Each year the boredom of inevitability, the predictable patterns of gastronomy, the echolalia of Christmas decorations, even the saminess of stars, he laments; the tautology of multicoloured porcelain birds-of-paradise, as light as feather, the white spotted death-cups swaying off the branch, the anniversary of small samovar bells. Because take the example of Faludy, he urges, and his ideal post-Cartesian man, the post-natal freedom, the absolution of nudity, the forgiveness of clotheslessness, the absolute absolution. A weightless stroll across woods of walls. No such thing as a short-cut between the thought and the said. Only the hollowed out name filled with outer space. Oh the lost substance of *homelands*. No need to tiptoe around buried bomb shells any more. It's winter solstice in the Northern glass. No such thing as border between the body and the ink. Nightfall, your garment, winged or wingless, clothes you with his or her own body. Don't be afraid, fearless *flâneur*. Keep the myrrh and the myth in the backpack of your old skin. A pocket knife, strings, extra pair of socks, a tiny ragged pair of winter gloves, a neon torch. Look, the diagnosis of this postmodern creature, he continues after swallowing a small poppy seed beijgli all in one, is named *tako tsubo*, a coronary syndrome when the organ's most important engine stops working and the heart all at once breaks. When this happens the left ventricle bulges out and resembles the shape of an octopus trapping Japanese fishing pot. Study the emotions' diseases which know nothing about the opaques of the heart. A final sip from the black espresso and the conversation ends with the blind dog's tale: last night he got entangled in the Christmas tree, carnage everywhere. Remains of red-beaked porcelain storks scattered around the entire country. No symbols where none intended.

The Death of Metal Goliaths

Another folio. The map of Derwent Edge (many gossip of). Peep through the half hourglass filled with this landscape and half emptied, the amphora of your centaur mind, and imagine this province overnight, when say, you were unremembering too, flooded and drained all at once. The simultaneous subsurface and over current of meanings. The heart's concave and convex shapes. The quagmire of sayings. Excavate the whereabouts of the two hundred dead pilots, the corroded carcasses of buried metal giants, the oxidized bell-clappers, the crooked spires swept away, the villages emerging from right under that lake, the phantom Wellingtons, the old Dakotas, the three hundred households with the three hundred drowned children. And vice versa. The once so static surfaces imploding under your foot, peat, sphagnum moss, histosol, limestone, black millstone grit, the springy soil, the lucky weather, blanket bog, the network of heather's thousand miniature roots. The entombment of anything we had. For the Devil's name uttered and numbed. The blue hare. Appearing and disappearing with the same speed of a random thought which knew nothing about its own speed. The rain that hurt skin. The numbered drinking basins carved out from sandstone to collect it. And then the atonement for all that made sense. The idle desire to belong in either direction.

Post Scriptum on Mute Bell Clappers

Those who could have begun the sentence have gone to bogland. With syntaxes which could have constructed a border between highlands and catacombs. Sometimes we are just so full of it; the relentless forecast of late October heat. The anguish. The displacement of seasons. They go so far as to call it Old Hags' summer. This means that the bill-clattering white storks will pay us an advance visit in the coming year prepared to nest on frozen chimneys to fight Arctic winds and snowstorms. This, they say, is the consequence of leaping fog.

A Conversation with Geraldine Monk's Owl

one midsummer night   she says   carrying a huge grey
bird on the sleeve of her mac   (darling – it's a barred owl
strix varia in *other* words) we saw a dark colossus descending
over *that* hedge   the silhouette of an old aeroplane   lights
on the wings each cabin lit up   flying so close to earth – to us
nearly touching the hair on our skull   that we thought it
was doomed to crash into the moors   I am sure   she adds
I saw what I saw   I *saw* propellers simultaneously still *and*
rotating   can you *imagine* she gesticulates with the globe-
eyed bird   claws caught in the coat   and not *only* that but
the-de-*de*-de fog moment when the giant faded   like people *do*
into forests or behind *moons* as quiet *as* a   mouse

Post Graffiti on Kelebia Wagons

In a way that everything absences. Budapest – Swab suburbia. Not much to remember here. You are always already gone elsewhere. Not much to forget. To recall the moment when you grew up. Dark coats retreat into dusk. No busy Brueghel winter market scene. You are here to feed the dogs, dig a tiny path in the snow, clear the factory yard of excrement and fill up bird feeders with sunflower seeds. One must wear at least two skins. And two gloves to do the job. And a pickaxe of your Achilles heels. Old snow is greyer underneath. Beauty is only in the snow of *now*, as it haloes the star-shaped goliath long knocked down from the roof. The outline of its fall, look, convex, hollow, comprehensible. And as it falls (when it fell), it falls down below towards the highway and lands right between the tracks and the old rail line by the river meandering quietly in the distance. And then *it*, like some estranged creature suddenly washed out into time, finally finds rest on rust right by the passing Kelebia Express (Number X of the Pan-European rail corridor), running up and down between the capital and the South, strolling through gravel mines, detouring into Andromeda fog. The territory of slow zones. The sovereignty of the still-born self. Head for new tracks of the circular mind. No such thing as absolute origo. Only the balkan desire to enter (exit) a world where cargo wagons pull in, in the end, the last depot of the continent. Where cargo wagons originate from. Where they'll once have unbecome. Szabadka. A postcard from a stranger. It's a landlet. *Peu de liberté.*

De Certeau's Night Webcam

An opaque night dice office space (recognizable) dusked up
books   what's left of them   in corners small bones of maps
used coffee cups the quadrangular life of a black box of one's
life electrochemical hums as if you were breathing   without
knowing   about the desire the lump of grey matter   the screen
titles all in gold the goliath's face lit   awful clarified   phantom
Franzstadt's traffic affairs tonight afar impersonal the derelict
chocolate factory (look) puffing away the smoke turning into
skyline   she pecks at your eyes   study the silence of *this* traffic
in hers   a tram shrieks as it forces its way along the bend of
the street as if changing the route on the track was labour as
if the routine hurt   the metallic noise of settling and unsettling
feathers bristling in the breeze   it's morning again   the night
peripatetic blinking the remains of a feral pigeon   flight feathers
just everywhere   a siren cries out the blue moon at aorta-level
maps of small bones the correspondence between the sheltered
the unsheltered the concave and convex the inside turned inside
out   four terracotta eggs the rattle of   fear-atlases falcon fluffs
just everywhere   peregrine mother tonight watch over us.

Post Scriptum on Snow and Cactus

The Christmas cactus flowered overnight. Magenta was just everywhere. Cracks in the walls got a thumb wider. But, the architect warns, you are safe, the sky won't fall down. Unnameable street is scaffolded securely on the world atlas. No such thing as fissure between the thought and the said. In the fibre of fears. Codices are delicate. Skin survives apocalypses caused by a turning page. Tonight winter has solsticed in the city. And snow just everywhere. All elements carry the same heavy fog weight, tons of ash. Study the consequence of the falling snow. What each breath, too, becomes. Say you could live with the mind of an hourglass, a tunnel engineer's thinking, the convex and concave form of being *here&there*. An old snow-plough sweeps across the winter evening. Creaking like old wars. You could always withdraw yourself from the map and once more, in a whiteout, become. You might go so far as to call it the sovereignty of saying, an unwanted one, but one, nonetheless.

Kelebia Express

And the vagabond of West Street, willowstick on back, feathers in hair, bells on hat, is always right in the end. Tiresome the not trying. Look to speak slowly. You are taking part in a walking race, she suggests. A mud path inwards, a frog's jump else(w) here. To and fro between two Novembers (oh you leapling). So that this to and froing can give birth to who(m). The desire for a narrative, growing, a metropolis, in either direction, she thinks. Because they say the greatest hazard is haste. The hour's inertia. The delay. Of the split second for the thought to become. Almost. Virtual. Even intimate. The melancholy of making. Love. Encyclopaedia. Habitat. The brutal pace of the turning of a page. How slow the rapid remembering. How leisurely one forgets. The tempo of talking. The dictionary of unknowing. In the crescendo of still-born sounds. The unhearing. The crawling of the Kelebia Express across the lack. The untimely calling at small town stops with random mad dogs on platforms, tails between legs. As if those werewolves were waiting for you. The resistance to arriving anywhere at all. Phantom stations along the edge. A personal blind map, soulless, peopleless. Orion. Andromeda. Centaur. The Moon. Study the anatomy of amnesia. The size of an iota, an omega. An empty fin-de-siècle pool. And in there, the marginalia. Summer echoes of changing rooms. And in there the clutter, the catatonia. First the falling. The forgetting, after. You could always tip the sand clock quickly upside down. The codex scorched. The agitato. Tons of ash flooding the mirror. No such thing as recognition between

now and its old reflection. Because it's not who runs. Here the
lessening air. Earth slows you down.

Post Scriptum

They've fledged.

Debts and Dedications

The book is a pocket map for Madeleine Callaghan and Paul O'Neill so that they will always know their way around.

For individual poems:

'The Sheffield Mágus': for Veronika Schandl and for the first stroll.

'Panorama from the Top of the Wicker Arches': for Richard De Ritter and for the second stroll.

'When Tremble and Tremor Turned up in Crookes': for Hungarian poet Gábor Nagy and for the Budapest friendship...

...& for Ethel Maqeda and for the Midsummer conversations in Crookes.

'The Carillonneur's Song': for the 'group-expedition' to Wardsend Cemetery and the Upperthorpe Project as part of Occursus.

'The Ornithologist': for the woodcarver of the Derbyshire woods.

'November Short-Cut': for Geraldine Monk and Alan Halsey and for the evening in the Stag. Without it (among other things), I would not have discovered Frog Lane.

'On the Cadence of Forgetting': for Denise Riley and for her one day-trip to Budapest.

'Post Scriptum on Symbols': for Győző Ferencz and for our Christmas conversation in Budapest.

'The Death of Metal Goliaths': for Louise. And I hereby certify that the 'drinking basins' mentioned in the poem can be found on Stanage Edge and not on Derwent Edge.

'De Certeau's Night Webcam': for Adam Piette and for armchair ornithology.

'Post Scriptum on Snow and Cactus': a homage to Edward Stachura.

'Post Graffiti on Kelebia Wagons': for my father and my grandfather. Szabadka's (now Subotica in Northern Serbia) French equivalent in the poem is the product of false etymologising.

The Tawny Owls in 'The Owls of Never Edge' were first spotted in Joanna Gavins' garden in Nether Edge, Sheffield in 2011.

And finally…

'Phantom Poems' for George and Mildred, the peregrine couple for sharing their precious family moments with the Sheffield Community via the University's Live Web Cam.

Acknowledgements

Many thanks for their continuing support to Adam Piette, Geraldine Monk, Alan Halsey, Denise Riley, Karen Solie, David Herd, Louise Johnson, Madeleine Callaghan, Paul O'Neill, Sokratis Kioussis, Kaarina Hollo, Nathan Hamilton, Zoe Skoulding, George Szirtes, Clarissa Upchurch, Sian Croose, Jo Budd, Henriette Louwerse and *citybooks*, Kate Kilalea, Anna Selby, Isabel Hill, Tessa Sowerby, Gábor Nagy, Noémi Kovács, Veronika Schandl, Gabriella Bazsó, Richard De Ritter, Andy Spragg, Ethel Maqeda, Fabienne Collignon, Gyöngyi Végh, the Hungarian Cultural Centre, London and my family and friends in Budapest.

Special thanks to Adam Piette, Louise Johnson and Richard De Ritter for their careful reading of the work in progress.

Many thanks to Tony Frazer and Shearsman Books for taking care of the manuscript in its various stages with attentiveness and precision.

Many thanks to designer and illustrator Judit Ferencz for her work on the cover design of the book.

Special thanks to Henriette Louwerse for commissioning the poems in 'Parasite of Town' for *citybooks* and to Nicky Hallett for the translation of modern texts into Middle English which appear in 'Postcard from West Street'.

A few of these poems, in earlier versions, have previously appeared in *Blackbox Manifold* (Issue 8), *citybooks*, UEA's *New Writing* (January, 2012), *Gathered Here Today* (Knives Forks and Spoons, 2012), *The Sheffield Anthology: Poems from the City Imagined* (Smith/Doorstop, 2012), *Dear World & Everyone in It* (Bloodaxe, 2013), *Drifting Down the Lane – Art & Poetry Explorations* (Moon and Mountain, 2013), *Rattapallax* (Issue 22), *The Missing Slate* (Autumn, 2013) and *Lighthouse Literary Journal* (Issue 4).

Poems in 'Parasite of Town' have been translated into Dutch by Hans Kloos and appeared in *citybooks* and in *Kluger Hans* (Autumn, 2011) in the Netherlands and into French by Michel Perquy, published in *citybooks*.

Lightning Source UK Ltd.
Milton Keynes UK
UKOW04f0823051215

264111UK00002B/51/P